Parenting Teenagers with Schizophrenia Disorder

Nurturing Resilience, Encouraging Growth, and Building a Supportive Family Environment for teens with Schizophrenia

Gerald M. Trexler

Table of Content

Introduction

Parenting teens is a difficult road, and when combined with the specific problems of schizophrenia disease, it gets much more complicated. Teens with schizophrenia present a unique set of challenges that need careful attention, sensitivity, and a personalized approach to parenting. This introduction intends to shed light on the many facets of parenting teens with schizophrenia disease, highlighting the need to build resilience, support development, and create a supportive family environment.

Schizophrenia illness in teens is a mental health problem marked by a variety of symptoms including hallucinations, delusions, disorganized thinking, and poor social functioning. Understanding the complexities of this condition is critical for parents navigating the complex landscape of adolescence while dealing with mental health issues. The path becomes a difficult balance between meeting a teenager's individual needs and giving the assistance required to manage schizophrenia.

Nurturing resilience takes center stage in this parental role since it entails developing the teenager's capacity to adapt, manage, and recover from the difficulties connected with schizophrenia. Resilience is not just a personal trait, but also a talent that can be improved and enhanced. In the setting of schizophrenia, developing resilience becomes critical to enabling youth to negotiate their particular experiences, establishing a feeling of agency, and improving general well-being.

The significance of promoting development in adolescents with schizophrenia cannot be emphasized. While the illness presents challenges, promoting development entails identifying and supporting the teen's unique qualities, abilities, and goals. This method not only helps to shape their identity but also lays the groundwork for a satisfying and meaningful life.

A supportive home environment emerges as a critical component in the path of parenting teens with schizophrenia. The family is the teen's major source of emotional, social, and practical support, determining their capacity to manage and prosper. Building this critical support system requires open communication, stigma reduction, and the provision of a secure and understanding environment within the family.

This introduction lays the groundwork for a thorough examination of tactics, insights, and concerns for developing resilience, supporting development, and creating a supportive family environment in negotiating the intricacies of parenting teens with schizophrenia illness.

Chapter 1: Understanding Schizophrenia during Adolescence

A. Characteristics and symptoms.

Understanding the features and symptoms of schizophrenia in adolescence is critical for parents navigating the complex terrain of raising teens with this condition. Schizophrenia is a serious mental health disorder that often appears in late adolescence or early adulthood. While symptoms vary in strength and appearance, they are commonly classified into three types: positive, negative, and cognitive symptoms.

Positive symptoms:

Adolescents with schizophrenia may have hallucinations, in which they see things that are not existent. These hallucinations might include auditory experiences, such as hearing voices.

Delusions: Teenagers with schizophrenia may have unreasonable thoughts or delusions. These ideas might be paranoid, grandiose, or weird, influencing their thoughts and actions. Negative symptoms include adolescent withdrawal from friends, family, and social activities.

Emotional Flatness: Teens with schizophrenia may exhibit a narrow range of emotions, seeming emotionally flat or disconnected.

Lack of Motivation: Common negative symptoms include a decline in the commencement of intentional tasks as well as a lack of motivation in general.

Cognitive symptoms:
Impaired Thinking: Adolescents may have disordered thinking, which makes it difficult to reason logically and articulate coherently.

Poor Executive Functioning: Common cognitive symptoms include difficulty making decisions, solving problems, and organizing activities.

Memory Impairment: Schizophrenia may impair both short-term and long-term memory, compromising academic achievement and everyday life.

Disorganized Symptoms:

Disorganized speaking: Teens may struggle to transmit ideas clearly, resulting in difficult-to-follow speaking patterns.

Disorganized Behavior: Unexpected or unexpected actions, such as incorrect emotional responses or unpredictable motions, might be detected.

Adolescents with schizophrenia may feel anxiety and depression, which may exacerbate their struggles.

Suicidal Thoughts: In certain circumstances, there may be an elevated risk of suicidal ideation or conduct.

Understanding these qualities and symptoms is critical for parents seeking to give appropriate assistance. Recognizing early warning indicators, such as changes in behavior, emotions, or social interactions, allows for earlier intervention, which may have a substantial influence on the course of the condition.

B. Diagnostics and Early Intervention

Diagnosing and intervening early in adolescence is critical when dealing with schizophrenia. Parents play an important role in identifying potential warning signals and getting expert treatment as soon as possible. Early indications may include social disengagement, scholastic deterioration, emotional or behavioral problems, and decreased cognitive function.

Mental health experts such as psychiatrists, psychologists, and social workers often conduct detailed evaluations to make a diagnosis. They analyze the teenager's background, family relationships, and observable behaviors. Brain imaging and psychological tests may also be used to get a definitive diagnosis.

Once identified, early intervention techniques use a multimodal approach. Medication management is often a critical component in relieving symptoms and stabilizing the youngster. Regular visits with psychiatrists allow you to check drug efficacy and change prescriptions as required.

Therapeutic therapies, such as cognitive-behavioral therapy (CBT) and family therapy, are critical for building resilience and development. CBT assists teenagers in managing unpleasant symptoms, while family therapy tackles the effect of schizophrenia on family relations by encouraging understanding and support.

Creating a supportive family environment entails open communication, information about schizophrenia, and empathy. Parents may work together with mental health specialists to create coping skills and crisis response plans. Establishing a routine and keeping a controlled, supportive environment helps to ensure stability.

Peer support groups and community resources are also essential for developing a thorough support system. Networking with other families going through similar issues may give vital insights and emotional support.

Chapter 2: Nurturing Resilience in Teens with Schizophrenia

A. Psychological approaches

Psychological treatments have an important role in developing resilience in adolescents with schizophrenia, therefore improving their general well-being. Here are the major tactics in this context:

Cognitive-behavioral therapy (CBT) effectively addresses erroneous cognitive processes and manages symptoms linked with schizophrenia.

Therapists assist teens in recognizing and fighting harmful ideas, as well as building coping techniques for everyday life issues.

The emphasis is on improving problem-solving abilities, communication, and self-awareness.

Educating youth and their families about schizophrenia is essential for eliminating stigma and increasing understanding.

Learning about the disorder's origin, symptoms, and treatment alternatives allows youth to actively engage in their care, which promotes a feeling of control.

Mindfulness-based interventions, including meditation and mindful breathing, may help kids manage stress and enhance their attention.

Mindfulness promotes self-acceptance and nonjudgmental awareness of thoughts and feelings, which aids in emotional management.

Adolescents with schizophrenia may struggle with social relations. Social skills training might help. Social skills training aims to improve communication, empathy, and relationship-building abilities.

Role-playing and real-life settings allow kids to practice and reinforce healthy social habits.

Strength-Based Approaches:

Identifying and developing the abilities and talents of teens with schizophrenia promotes a feeling of competence and self-esteem.

Recognizing successes, no matter how minor, promotes a good self-image and builds resilience.

Family therapy involves the whole family, which improves communication and understanding.

Family members learn how to effectively assist the adolescent, provide a controlled atmosphere, and resolve any problems.

Resilience-Focused treatments:
These treatments attempt to improve resilience by promoting coping mechanisms and adaptive techniques.
Therapists collaborate with teenagers to uncover personal strengths and create resilience-building activities.
Peer support and group therapy may help teens with schizophrenia feel more connected and understood.
Group therapy settings enable people to share their experiences and learn from others who are dealing with similar issues.

In summary, psychological methods for parenting teens with schizophrenia include a wide range of treatments, education, and support networks aimed at fostering resilience, supporting development, and creating a supportive home environment. These solutions help kids handle the intricacies of their disease and live fulfilled lives.

B. Developing Emotional Strength.

Building emotional strength in adolescents with schizophrenia is an important part of developing resilience and supporting overall well-being. Here are special parenting practices for teens with schizophrenia:

Emotional Regulation Techniques:
Teach teenagers practical skills for controlling their emotions.

Deep breathing, mindfulness, and gradual muscular relaxation may all help individuals deal with stress and emotional swings.

Validate and empathize with teens to create a positive home atmosphere.

Demonstrate empathy and active listening, emphasizing that their feelings are noticed and accepted without judgment.

Promote open and honest communication among family members for therapeutic purposes.

Create a secure environment for adolescents to communicate their ideas and feelings, therefore fostering trust and improving the parent-child connection.

Expressive Arts Therapy:

Encourage teenagers to express themselves via art or music therapy.

Creative activities may be effective instruments for expressing feelings and cultivating a sense of success.

Encouraging Self-Reflection:

Help youth reflect on their feelings and experiences.

Journaling and other self-reflective hobbies may help you get a better knowledge of your strengths and weaknesses.

Collaborate with mental health providers to create a crisis intervention strategy.

Provide teenagers with coping methods and a clear strategy for obtaining assistance during difficult times, giving them a feeling of control over their mental health.

Good reinforcement involves recognizing and reinforcing good actions and coping techniques.

Celebrate little accomplishments, creating a pleasant atmosphere that enables teenagers to develop their emotional strengths.

Creating a Support Network:
Connect with peers who understand and support the teen's experience.

A solid support network, which includes friends, family, and mental health specialists, helps to boost emotional resilience.

Introduce mindfulness activities to help teenagers focus on the present moment.

Mindful activities, such as guided meditation or mindful walking, may improve mental health and decrease anxiety.

Encourage independence by gradually empowering youth to manage their everyday lives.

Encouraging independence instills a feeling of success and confidence in their abilities to overcome obstacles.

Chapter 3: Promoting Growth and Development

A. Educational Support.

Educational assistance is critical in promoting growth and development for teens with Schizophrenia Disorder, especially in the setting of parenthood. Understanding the particular issues associated with schizophrenia is critical for parents, schools, and support groups.

To increase knowledge and awareness, parents should get a thorough education about schizophrenia, its symptoms, and its effect on youth. This understanding helps parents to spot warning signals, sympathize with their child's difficulties, and react accordingly.

Educational assistance provides parents with practical tools for efficient communication with their adolescents. Learning how to manage problematic behaviors and promote good relationships is critical for creating a healthy family environment.

Coping skills: Parents may acquire coping skills to negotiate the emotional complexity of parenting a teenager with schizophrenia. This involves stress management, self-care, and seeking outside assistance when required.

Advocacy and Collaboration: Educational programs should prioritize advocating for the needs of teens with schizophrenia in the school system. Collaboration among parents, schools, and mental health specialists is critical to ensuring a comprehensive support framework.

Parents may learn how to help their adolescents develop resilience. Instead of concentrating primarily on the obstacles, parents can promote a positive outlook, encourage problem-solving skills, and emphasize their child's talents and possibilities.

Educational assistance for teens with schizophrenia should include knowledge of various treatment approaches and how they benefit their general well-being. This encompasses cognitive-behavioral therapy, family therapy, and pharmaceutical management.

To build a supportive home environment, parents might establish routines, set realistic expectations, and foster open communication. A secure and understanding home environment is critical for the development of adolescents with schizophrenia.

Encouraging parents to connect with support groups and community services is essential. These relationships allow you to share your experiences, learn ideas, and establish a network of others who understand the particular difficulties of parenting an adolescent with schizophrenia.

B. Social Integration Strategies

Social integration tactics are critical for promoting the growth and development of teens with Schizophrenia Disorder while also encouraging resilience in the home setting. Here are some thorough suggestions for parents in this setting.

Educate the community about schizophrenia to decrease stigma and promote understanding. This might lead to the youngster receiving more acceptance and support from the community.

Collaborate with schools to establish inclusion initiatives that foster understanding between peers and instructors. Workshops, lectures, and awareness campaigns may all contribute to a more friendly school climate.

Facilitate peer support groups in the community or school context. These clubs may provide teens with schizophrenia a feeling of belonging by establishing empathy and connections with peers who face similar struggles.

Encourage youngsters to pursue extracurricular activities based on their interests. This not only improves their abilities and confidence but also makes social interactions easier, encouraging a feeling of normality.

Involve family members in social events to create a support network. This might involve going to community events, joining groups, or attending social gatherings where the adolescent feels included and welcomed.

Provide communication skills training to parents and teens. Effective communication is essential for managing social situations and improving abilities may lead to stronger connections with classmates and family members.

Gradual exposure to social circumstances is recommended, taking into account the teenager's degree of comfort. This step-by-step strategy promotes confidence and resilience, reducing the potential stress involved with social encounters.

Mentorship Programs: Pair teens with schizophrenia with mentors for advice, support, and understanding. This mentoring may go outside the family, providing new insights and encouragement.

Explore online support networks and forums to connect with other adolescents and parents experiencing similar issues. This virtual support network may provide guidance, share experiences, and foster a feeling of community.

Create crisis intervention strategies for complex social circumstances. Give both parents and teens techniques for dealing with future crises and making sure they feel prepared to face challenging situations.

Advocacy Training: Teach parents and teens about self-advocacy. This involves recognizing their rights, expressing their needs, and obtaining adjustments as needed to provide a feeling of control and empowerment.

By employing these social integration tactics, parents may actively help the growth and development of teens suffering from schizophrenia disorder. These efforts not only build resilience but also create a supportive family atmosphere that spreads across the community, fostering inclusion and understanding.

Chapter 4: Building a Supportive Family Environment

A. Communication Techniques.

Open and Honest Communication:

Create an atmosphere in which open and honest communication is encouraged. Encourage family members to freely share their opinions and emotions, which will develop trust and understanding.

Psychoeducation: Help family members understand schizophrenia better. This information enables them to give greater assistance, minimize stigma, and foster a more empathic environment.

Practice active listening with teenagers. This includes paying full attention, respecting their emotions, and reacting intelligently. It develops the feeling of being heard and understood.

Develop empathy and compassion within your family. Recognize the specific obstacles that a kid with schizophrenia faces, and react with compassion and understanding. This contributes to the development of an emotionally supportive atmosphere.

Establishing a steady schedule may give stability for teenagers. Predictability in everyday routines may aid with symptom management and stress reduction. Involve the adolescent in developing and sustaining this regimen.

Use positive reinforcement to recognize and reward favorable actions. This method promotes the development of adaptive behaviors and fosters feelings of achievement.

Consider family therapy as a means to solve difficulties together. Therapeutic therapies may assist family members in better understanding their responsibilities, improving communication, and learning appropriate coping skills.

Set realistic objectives for teenagers based on their strengths and limits. This fosters a feeling of achievement while avoiding needless pressures that might aggravate symptoms.

Teach and practice healthy conflict resolution techniques within your family. Provide members with techniques for constructively resolving conflicts, eliminating possible sources of stress for the adolescent.

Individualized Support Plans: Create support plans tailored to the teenager's needs and preferences. This individualized approach guarantees that the family atmosphere is designed to promote their well-being.

Encourage independence by gradually enabling teenagers to take on responsibility. This promotes confidence and a feeling of control over their lives, which contributes to overall resilience.

To prepare for a crisis, create a plan outlining procedures to follow during an emergency or symptom escalation. Preparedness minimizes worry for both the adolescent and the family, resulting in a safer atmosphere.

By using these communication tactics and practices, families may help teens with schizophrenia develop resilience, mature, and create a supportive atmosphere. Remember that consistency and continued assistance are essential in treating this difficult disease.

B. Establishing Routine and Stability.

Establish a regular daily schedule with established hours for getting up, food, activities, and bedtime. This regularity helps the youngster feel more stable, lowering worry and tension.

Involve the adolescent in planning and developing a routine. This instills a feeling of control and ownership, making them more inclined to stick to the timetable.

Maintain a balanced schedule by including educational, recreational, and self-care activities. This variation promotes general well-being and avoids boredom.

Prioritize Sleep Hygiene: Highlight the significance of proper sleep hygiene. Establish a regular nighttime routine to encourage excellent sleep, which is essential for treating schizophrenia symptoms.

Maintain structure, but also allow for flexibility. Recognizing that unexpected occurrences may occur, and being adaptive allows the family to manage transitions more easily.

Schedule frequent family gatherings to review and adapt routines together. This guarantees that everyone's wants and preferences are addressed, fostering a feeling of collaboration.

Establish clear expectations for everyday duties and tasks. This precision lowers misunderstanding and gives the adolescent a feeling of duty within the family unit.

Integrate therapeutic activities into daily routines, such as counseling, medication management, or support groups. This reflects the family's concern for the teenager's mental wellbeing.

Encourage self-care habits as part of daily routines. This might include mindfulness exercises, relaxation methods, or activities that improve emotional well-being.

Recognize and appreciate successes, no matter how minor. Positive reinforcement within the routine increases the teenager's feeling of achievement and self-esteem.

Use visual aids, such as timetables or calendars, to enforce routines. Visual clues may assist people with schizophrenia in comprehending and following an organized strategy.

Collaborative Decision-Making: Involve teenagers in ordinary decisions. This engagement empowers them and instills a feeling of agency in their everyday lives.

Integrating crisis preparation into routines involves determining particular steps to perform when anticipated problems. This proactive strategy guarantees that the family is prepared to manage unanticipated occurrences.

Families may help their loved one develop resilience and create a supportive atmosphere by developing a routine that promotes stability and takes into account the special requirements of an adolescent with schizophrenia.

Chapter 5: Collaboration with Healthcare Professionals.

A. The role of mental health experts

Comprehensive Assessment:
Mental health specialists work alongside healthcare professionals to undertake a thorough evaluation of the teenager's mental health, taking into account both psychological and medical factors. This coordinated effort provides a comprehensive awareness of each individual's demands.

Individualized Treatment Programs: Mental health specialists collaborate with healthcare providers to create tailored treatment programs for schizophrenia-specific difficulties. This strategy might involve a mix of medication, therapy, and other therapeutic approaches.

Mental health professionals play an important role in teaching families about schizophrenia and its effects on teens. This joint effort ensures that healthcare providers and families are properly informed, supporting a cohesive approach to assistance.

Coordination of Care: Mental health specialists and healthcare professionals collaborate to guarantee effective communication and treatment options. This cooperation increases the efficacy of therapies.

Collaboration between mental health specialists and healthcare professionals may lead to effective family therapy sessions. These sessions are focused on enhancing communication, resolving family difficulties, and creating a supportive atmosphere for the adolescent.

Pharmaceutical management involves collaboration between mental health specialists and healthcare professionals to monitor and change pharmaceutical regimens. This coordination ensures that the drug regimen is in line with the overall therapy objectives.

Mental health specialists work with healthcare professionals to create crisis response strategies. This involves specifying the measures to be performed in the event of an acute episode, guaranteeing a proactive and coordinated response.

Regular Progress Reviews: Mental health specialists and healthcare professionals collaborate to examine the success of treatment plans for teenagers. Adjustments may be made to meet the teenager's developing demands.

Mental health specialists collaborate with healthcare professionals to provide skills training for teenagers and their families. Coping tactics, communication skills, and stress-management approaches may all be included.

Collaboration involves combining community resources to assist teenagers' well-being. Mental health specialists and healthcare professionals collaborate to link families with appropriate support networks.

Mental health specialists urge a comprehensive approach to treatment, addressing not just the symptoms of schizophrenia but also its emotional and social impact. This lobbying provides a more complete and tailored treatment plan.

Mental health specialists and healthcare professionals collaborate on community education and awareness programs to decrease stigma and enhance understanding and empathy toward schizophrenia.

B. Medication Management: Initial Assessment and Diagnosis.

The partnership starts with a comprehensive evaluation by healthcare professionals and mental health specialists to diagnose schizophrenia. This examination guides the creation of an appropriate medication management strategy.

Healthcare providers work with mental health specialists to recommend drugs that address the teenager's symptoms and requirements. The selection process takes into account the medication's effectiveness as well as possible negative effects.

Educating Families: Healthcare professionals and mental health specialists collaborate to educate families about prescription drugs. This covers dose information, possible adverse effects, and the significance of following the drug plan.

Ongoing cooperation requires frequent monitoring of the teenager's reaction to medicine. Healthcare specialists collaborate with mental health experts to make required modifications, resulting in the most effective and well-tolerated therapy.

Effective communication between healthcare providers and mental health specialists is essential for addressing medication-related side effects and concerns. This partnership enables timely modifications or alternate techniques as required.

Incorporating non-pharmacological approaches:
Collaboration goes beyond drugs and includes non-pharmacological treatments like therapy and skill training. The ultimate objective is to develop a comprehensive treatment plan that addresses both the medical and psychological elements of schizophrenia.

Collaborative medication management engages teenagers and their families in decision-making. Informed consent and active participation provide a feeling of collaboration throughout the treatment process.

Regular Medication Reviews: Healthcare professionals and mental health specialists collaborate to analyze the medication plan's efficacy. This joint review informs any changes required to improve the teenager's well-being.

Mental health specialists educate teens and their families about the significance of medication compliance. Understanding the advantages improves adherence to the suggested regimen.

Collaboration is crucial in building crisis intervention strategies for medication management. Clear processes are created to deal with any emergency crises, providing a coordinated response from healthcare professionals and mental health specialists.

Medication management is linked with therapy sessions facilitated by mental health professionals.

This teamwork guarantees a comprehensive treatment, treating both physiological and psychological concerns via medicines and therapy approaches.

Healthcare professionals and mental health specialists collaborate to provide families with community support and services that complement medication management. This includes support groups, educational initiatives, and other services that help to create a helpful atmosphere.

By using a collaborative and integrated approach to medication management, healthcare professionals and mental health specialists may help teens with schizophrenia develop resilience, thrive, and construct a supportive home environment.

Chapter 6: Legal and Ethical Considerations

A. Advocating for Teens with Schizophrenia.

Advocating for teens with schizophrenia entails negotiating legal and ethical issues to guarantee that their rights and well-being are protected. Legal frameworks differ, but it is critical to grasp laws governing mental health, confidentiality, and education.

Informed permission and Confidentiality: Ensure teens may provide informed permission for treatment and participate in legal choices.

Advocate for strong confidentiality safeguards to preserve sensitive information, while balancing the need to include parents or guardians.

Learn about special education legislation, such as the Individuals with Disabilities Education Act (IDEA), to provide adequate services and accommodations.

Work to develop Individualized Education Plans (IEPs) that are customized to the specific requirements of adolescents with schizophrenia.

Advocate for appropriate mental health care, including therapy, medication, and support services. Address any hurdles, such as insurance limits or gaps in services.

Learn about anti-discrimination legislation, such as the Americans with Disabilities Act (ADA), to prohibit discrimination based on mental health status in education, employment, and public services.

Balance youth with schizophrenia's right to make treatment decisions with parental participation, especially if there are concerns about their competence to make educated choices.

Understanding the legal processes for involuntary hospitalization or involvement during a crisis is crucial for ensuring the safety of the adolescent and others around them while preserving their rights.

Advocate for minors in court procedures by partnering with mental health law experts.

Community Integration: Encourage teens with schizophrenia to participate in social and recreational activities while minimizing stigma and increasing acceptance.

Consider cultural competence while advocating for mental health concerns, since cultural elements may impact how they are seen and treated within families and communities.

Maintain ethical limits while advocating for teens, respecting their autonomy and privacy, and balancing the importance of parental engagement and support.

Overall, advocating for youth with schizophrenia requires a thorough awareness of legal frameworks, ethical principles, and coordination with mental health doctors, educators, and legal experts to guarantee the best possible results for all parties involved.

B. Ensure Access to Resources

Ensuring access to services while parenting teens with Schizophrenia Disorder requires a comprehensive strategy that includes legal and ethical issues. Here is a comprehensive exploration:

Legal considerations:

Healthcare Rights: Learn about the legal rights of people with mental health issues, such as schizophrenia. This involves receiving adequate healthcare, drugs, and treatment.

Educational Rights: Understand your teenager's educational rights. The Individuals with Disabilities Education Act (IDEA) of the United States, for example, assures that students with disabilities, including mental health disorders, get a free and appropriate education.

Privacy laws: Respect your teen's privacy while balancing the need to share information within the family and with healthcare experts. Familiarize yourself with relevant privacy legislation, such as the Health Insurance Portability and Accountability Act.

Ethical considerations:

Autonomy and Informed Consent: Respect your teenager's autonomy. Involve them in treatment decisions, taking into account their ability to grant informed consent. Strive for collaborative decision-making with healthcare providers.

Cultural Competence: Understand the cultural context of parenting and mental health. Consider cultural ideas, attitudes, and traditions while developing a treatment plan to ensure that it is culturally competent and responsive.

Non-Discrimination: Maintain the principles of nondiscrimination. Ensure that your adolescent has fair and equal access to services, regardless of their mental health status, and speak out against stigmatization.
Access to resources:

Mental Health treatments: Locate and use mental health treatments geared to youth with schizophrenia. Adolescent mental health specialists include psychiatrists, psychologists, and counselors.

Community Support: Look into community resources such as support groups for parents and teens with schizophrenia. Connecting with people who have had similar situations may give helpful insights and emotional support.

Educational Support: Work with educators and school officials to provide the necessary modifications for your kid. This might include an Individualized Education Program (IEP) or a 504 plan.

Financial Assistance: Look into possible financial assistance programs or grants that might help teens with schizophrenia pay for treatment and support services.

Creating a supportive family environment:

Communication: Encourage open and honest communication within the family. Encourage your youngster to talk about his or her emotions, struggles, and triumphs with their illness.

Education and Awareness: Educate family members about schizophrenia to foster understanding and empathy. This contributes to the creation of a supportive atmosphere, reducing the likelihood of misunderstandings.

Resilience-Building Activities: Incorporate resilience-building activities into family life. This might include mindfulness exercises, stress-reduction strategies, and regular family activities that foster connection.

Chapter 7: Case Studies and Success Stories

A. Real-world examples of Positive Outcomes

Developing coping strategies: To handle their teen's symptoms, the family used open communication and problem-solving approaches on a constant basis. Over time, the adolescent developed appropriate coping skills, decreasing the burden of schizophrenia in their everyday lives.

Building a Supportive Network: By actively participating with support groups and mental health specialists, a family built a strong support network. This network offered both emotional and practical assistance, allowing the youngster and their family to face the problems of schizophrenia together.

Encouraging Independence: A family gradually pushed their youngster to take on more responsibility and make choices about their treatment plan. This allowed the kid to take control of their situation and develop a feeling of independence and self-confidence.

Celebrating Achievements: A family recognized their teenager's little successes and milestones, reinforcing good habits and building self-esteem. This positive reinforcement encouraged the youngster to continue their path of development and perseverance, despite the difficulties provided by schizophrenia.

Promoting Wellness: By emphasizing self-care activities like exercise, good diet, and mindfulness, a family helped their adolescent manage their symptoms and preserve their overall well-being. This comprehensive strategy improved the teenager's stability and resilience in dealing with schizophrenia.

B. Lessons Learned From Challenges

Patience is essential when dealing with schizophrenia in teens. Understanding that development may be gradual and setbacks may occur is critical for creating a supportive workplace.

Flexibility in Parenting Styles: Traditional parenting practices may need to be modified to meet the specific demands of an adolescent with schizophrenia. Flexibility in parenting approaches may aid in efficiently managing symptoms and promoting resilience.

Communication: It is critical to maintain open and honest communication within the family unit. Encourage communication regarding emotions, symptoms, and worries to better understand the teen's point of view and create trust.

Seeking Professional Guidance: It is critical to identify when more assistance is required and to seek advice from mental health providers. They may provide helpful insights, therapy alternatives, and coping skills based on the teenager's individual requirements.

Caregivers should prioritize self-care while caring for a teenager with schizophrenia. Caregivers must prioritize their own mental and physical health in order to adequately assist their adolescents and avoid fatigue.

Appreciating small Victories: Recognizing and appreciating even minor accomplishments may increase a teenager's confidence and drive. This positive reinforcement may promote long-term development and resilience.

Building a Support Network: It is critical to establish a robust support network that includes family, friends, support groups, and mental health experts. Having a community that understands and empathizes with the difficulties may be quite beneficial to both the adolescent and their family.

CONCLUSION

To summarize, parenting teens with schizophrenia requires a multidimensional strategy focused on building resilience, supporting personal development, and creating a supportive family environment. Key tactics include open communication, comprehension, and participation in therapeutic procedures. By fostering resilience, parents may help their teenagers negotiate the obstacles of schizophrenia while also boosting self-esteem and independence.

Looking forward, teenagers with schizophrenia may have a bright future thanks to continued advances in medical science and mental health assistance. The combination of novel therapies, community services, and educational opportunities creates a hopeful environment for these people to live productive lives. Furthermore, ongoing family participation and activism help to break down social stigmas around mental health, paving the way for a more inclusive and understanding society.

Parenting teens with schizophrenia needs determination, tolerance, and a commitment to continuous learning. By adopting these tactics and having a positive attitude, parents may play an important part in crafting a better future for their teenagers, helping them to flourish despite the obstacles offered by schizophrenia.

Self Reflection Questions

How have your communication skills improved in order to establish an open and understanding discourse with your adolescent who has been diagnosed with schizophrenia?

In what ways have you actively sought to help your adolescent develop resilience and a good self-image despite the obstacles of schizophrenia?

What particular tactics have you used to support personal development and independence in your schizophrenic teenager?

How has your home environment changed to be more helpful and conducive to the well-being of your adolescent with schizophrenia?

How has schooling influenced your family's path, and how can you improve your knowledge of schizophrenia to better help your teenager?

____

____

____

____

In what ways have you used external resources, such as support groups or mental health specialists, to help your family's coping techniques and strategies?

____

____

____

____

How can you strike a balance between providing a controlled atmosphere for your schizophrenic adolescent and enabling them to express themselves individually and freely?

____

____

____

____

What problems have you had in breaking down cultural stigmas around mental health in your family, and how can you continue to confront and overcome them?

____

How has your personal resilience been challenged throughout your parenting experience, and which self-care methods have been most beneficial in keeping you healthy?

Looking forward, what particular aims or expectations do you have for your family in terms of supporting your teenager's development and resilience with schizophrenia?